DONALD?
DUCK OR
GOD'S TRUMP
CARD

Based on revelation in 1994

TRANSCRIBED
BY G. D. PHILLIPS

G. D. PHILLIPS

DONALD?
DUCK OR GOD'S
TRUMP CARD

AUTHOR

G. D. PHILLIPS & GRACEIA GOLD

Publisher Goldendtruth Publications.

Copyright © 2016 G. D. PHILLIPS

ISBN-13:978-1540306982

ISBN-10:1540306984

G. D. PHILLIPS

Prosper Where You Are!

DEDICATION

In dedication to YOU.

WHY?
So you're free to Re-Right life in harmony.

ACKNOWLEDGMENTS

Grateful to Truth: You came when we called.

ACKNOWLEDGEMENT

Much thanks to all who ask
Much thanks to all who learn
Much thanks to all who live
Much thanks to all who died!

NOW?
May wrongs, be nil and nullified
May thoughts, be pure and purified
May hearts, be soft and unified.

May minds reset and hurts unwind
May lives be loved and men be kind
May slaves be loosed and lives rewind

May Judge and Jury uphold Love's Laws
May War and conflict, heed Joy's call
May Freedom's cloak, be worn by all.

May Peace and Joy rule and reign
May the government of Love begin again
May Harmony's path be clear and plain
So the Silenced Lamb is freed from
pain.

CONTENTS

CHAPTER 1
TRUMP CARD

"How can a nation change in a day?' I ask.

"Is my arm too short to save: I can. I say so!"
The Voice responds strongly.

"Watch: Trump will win"
'Trump? Why will Trump win?' I ask, mildly.

"Because Donald is hillarious. They'll think he's a joker in the pack, a quacking Duck: But I'll show them: I'll show them God's still in control: I confound the wisdom of the wise: I'll confound the wise men in smart suits. I'll show them that Donald is God's Trump card".

God's words in January 1994
G. D. PHILLIPS
Witness.

VISION: CAN A NATION CHANGE IN 1 DAY

Faces upon faces! Frightened faces, freezing in fear. Faces of failure, stress, strain: So many people, multitudes in the valleys of in-decision

'It's Incredulous! It looks like America: It looks like Civil War' I shout out loud. It's incredulous!

It's January 1994. We're in London. I'm watching a picture of turmoil, playing in empty space, in my living room.

A Voice like the sound of all creation fills my ears. Yet The Voice speaks like a lover speaks to his wife. Calm yet the voice carries the authority of a billion kings.

Suddenly I realize, it's a vision. It's an open vision of the future: I see all of America, arising; every one alarmed or armed!

CHAPTER 2

FOOLISH TRUMP WILL WIN 2016

Suddenly, I see all of America,
arising and alarmed or armed!

God's words repeated for summer 2016
G. D. PHILLIPS - Witness.

"" I will take the foolish things of this world and use them to confound the wise ones. Look and See: I will take a fool and make him King. I will take the foolish thing; and confound the wise.

Hilary is wise. Hilary is the 'wise' choice. Yet I Am God of all the earth: I who confound the wise, I am all around and Yes I AM still here. No matter who 'thinks' they got rid of me!

Those who 'think' and are busy 'thinking'? Let them THINK!

They think there is no God: They think God is dead: They think God is bad: But watch! They're about to be confounded. They're about to be confounded again.

Think, isn't it all they can do? Can they make rain or soil, wind or snow, grain or gold? Can they make toes or fingers, moons or stars, fire or water? Can a man save a man from final death. Let him *Think* he can!

So what: Who makes the river run or the sun burn. Who turns neutrons or electrons? Who makes your Higson Boson particles. Think?

They think they can throw stones to the moon, dig holes to the core; so they feel powerful, rational, logical! It's all explainable.

They think, so I too will 'think' Lets see,

whose 'thinking' has more power. Them or me!

Hence right now, 'I think' I will play my Trump card. I will take a wild card out of no where and make it into the top card. I will take the joker out of the pack and play it as my King card. I will take The bottom card and I will make it become the top card. I will make The fool into The King.

Why am I acting? Why am I intervening? Why? So that you'll know it's me. I am acting, so you sit up and take note. I am acting because your days are numbered. Yes, YOUR days are numbered, you doubters. So you can not ignore me anymore: So you will not dismiss me much longer.

Why? Because you need to listen: Earth needs to listen. I AM COMING FOR YOU.""

CHAPTER 3
WHAT'S IN A NAME!

Suddenly, I see all of America,
arising and alarmed; or armed!

Seriously, what's in a name? Is it an accident?
Just coincidence? Or an identity to match the
blueprints on earth. What's a name got to do
with your destiny; with who, on earth, you are.

WHO ON EARTH ARE YOU!
Now who on earth is this Donald?
And who on earthy is this Hilary? And why on
earth are they here at such a time as this! It's
not over yet. The battle's just begun!

DID YOU KNOW
Did you know Hilary means hilarious! It also
means cheerful but it can be hilariously

negative or hilariously positive. What is
History saying? Happy Hilary or Hilarious
Hilary! Dumb Donald or Dominant Donald!
Now who on earth is this Donald?
And why on earth is he here at such a time as
this!

*Righteousness is here to stay. so you better get
purified and beautified if you wish to survive!*

CHAPTER 4

WHAT'S GOD'S COMPLAINT

Suddenly, I see all of America,
arising and alarmed or armed!

GOD'S COMPLAINT
""You can not charge ahead with war any more: Making war on the un-armed, making war on the unwaged, war on the unsaved, war on the out-raged. War war war.

You who gag the defenders of the weak; You who silence those with No voice: You who champion offenders; You who make wrong things right.
Leave my children alone: Leave The Peaceful in peace: Let them be.
Do not disturb their calm.

Do not disturb their peace.

WITH WHAT

With your advertising, broadcasting False-Broadcasts-Television! Showing 'goods' which I call 'bads': Those products and services which tell a lie. Instead these deception machines, are meal-disruption mechanisms, stopping people from eating rightly, stpping families from staying together and praying together. Forcing people to order 'Fast Foods' which are trully 'Fats Foods'.

Pedalling misery as drugs and pills. Pharmaceuticals rulling and reigning in the land through advertising.   Addicting my children to your mixed up poisons. You think I do not see? You think I do not see you Mr Pharmacy? I am watching you Mr Pharmacy.

I am watching as you use pills and posions to disable my kids. In a few years time, the thing you call medicine, now, prescribes sickness later: Perforating their defence system; punching their immunity; initiating cancer, blood pressure sickness, diabetes, heart disease.

You vaccine them for your own good: Not theirs. Pocketing money, by producing poxins. Poxins: Toxins indeed! Feeding animal serum into my human beings. How degrading. How be-littling, how dishonouring of my creation. I made them. I am their Father. Their True Father.

I hate my children suffering:

Creation's kids suffering from lack of vision, from lack of wisdom! Suffering lack of sunshine and lack of vitamins, lack of minerals, lack of calcioum for strong teeth, strong bones. To make their bones weak, you deprive them f my light: My children sit in offices in concrete blocks of imprisonment. You're imprisoning their freedom. You harvest their intellect to harness power for you.

You're imprisoning their creativity: You're inhibiting their ability to play; I sent them to play, not labour under slavery's yokes and burdens. See! I see you Mr Pharmacy. I see you Miss Education.

I am watching as you wreck havoc with my natural order, I am watching as you genetically modify my crops, I am watching as you turn electricity into your power-god. I am watching as you move millions on millions into dependency on power; Power that WILL fail! into light that will kill. I am watching you Mister Electricity. I am watching you.

My Trump card will do as I will. It will confound the wise. I will use it to blow away cobwebs of dispair. I will use it to wedge the door open on your dirty politics. I will use it to expose the corruption you hide in brown paper packets. I will use it to expose the Inside of your party-political packs of power.

Deals that give Pharmaceutical companies power to send 13 year olds to cancer wards. Deals that give Tobacco companies license to freely kill my kids. Deals that give electricity companies power to starve my kids, from fuel for heating, of fuel for cooking, while the fat bums grow rich and big.

I will ransack your Brown paperbag deals that send Big Farmer to plaster sacred lands with pesticides, fertilisers, weed killers / plant killers,bug killers, insect killers, life killers! Life-Killers; killing the life in the food and bringing death in to the eaters."

I am moving in. I am here to stay. I am here to reign. I will save my kids. I am the Originator. I will save you all.   You who love me. Listen. I am reaching in, will you be rescued.""

CHAPTER 5

DON ALD - BATTLE BEFORE TRIUMPH

Suddenly, I see all of America,
arising and alarmed or armed!

DON
Don:- King, dominion, sovereign, dominant, dumb, dumb founded, donamatrix, madona, and that's all before we get to the 'ald'.

ALD
Ald, all, scald, bald, fauld, mauld, world. Donald is a strong name. Famous name, think of Donalds. How dominating are they? famous even, even as a duck: DONALD DUCK!

RULER

Watch this: Donald is From the Gaelic name
Domhnall which means guess what?.. RULER!
More precisely it means "ruler of the world",
Donald is composed of the old Celtic
elements dumno "world" and val "rule". Two
9th-century kings of the Scots and Picts
famously named.

Trump's middle name is the English derivative
of the Hebrew name, Yohanan, which means
Graced by Yahweh. Hilary too!

Grace is very important in this new age. Did
you know 'The Age of Grace' is here? What
does the Age Of Grace mean? Every one,
every where, every time has gone wrong or
felt wrong. The Age of Grace is about
cancellation / Un-doing of wrong.

Simple Physics says: For every action there is a
reaction: For every push, there is a pull. and
for every up there is a down... Simple Physics
tells you that:

To every wrong there is a right.

To every sin there is payback.

To every crime there is a punishment.

Simple.

Use the gift of this Grace Age to end what's wrong and start what's right.

Suddenly, I see all of America,
arising and alarmed or armed!

This name Trump; does it mean America is coming out trumps?! Good news is: This winning Trump means a winning America! YES. It is a sign.

Of course you'll have to go through the battle to get the victory but it's definitely a time for winning. But it's also a time for winning for every thing, that will shape the world into harmony. It's a winning time for everthing that will sweep the American political house clean!

CLEAN UP

But who knows that to clean a house, you
need to sweep a house? For a house to be
clean, you got to sweep the house clean.

DIRT MUST GO

Yes, dirt will go. Rubbish will be tossed out.
Mould scrubbed away. Grime removed. Trash
taken out. Crap churned and burned. This is
the times we are in.

CHAPTER 6
CLEANING YOUR MOTIONS

Suddenly, I see all of America,
arising and alarmed or armed!

If you are going to win, you're going to need
Self - Control. Hold your self in control now;
and you'll win the battle in the long run. Start
disciplining your life now and you'll disperse
the traps that so easily beset you.

PURIFY
Purify your life right now and you'll begin to
enjoy life according to purity and
righteousness. No one will lie to you. No one
will steal from you. No one will sabotage your
work. No one will interfere with your children.

NO MESS
No one will mess up your legacy and no one
will mess with your partner your lover or your
business. What ever belongs to you will come
under the powerful power for righteousness.
You will be rich and right. Rich and right: No
other position is better than this!

SOLUTIONS NOT EMOTIONS
No more the old ways where the down right
dirty and the damned have the upper hand.
The wheel of life is turning. As you turn to
right-living, right living will come. As you turn
away from disharmony, harmony will come.
Because the age of Harmony has come.

GRACE AND HARMONY
That is why Hilary and Donald both have
names that imply 'GRACE'. Both names
borrow their meaning from Grace: Meaning
the blessed one; meaning 'gifted': Meaning the
gift of grace.

Grace brings with it's righteousness. Grace is the pre-cursor to 'harmony'. Before Grace there is 'Light'. But before Light, there is 'Word'. (or Sound). And what is Wird / Sound? Sound is all the movement of thoughts in the world.

Before sound (or Word) there is God. God is the originator of thought. God thought out all the beautiful plans for all the beauty-full people in the world.

MAN UN-THINKS GOD'S PLAN
By the way, it is man that 'un-thinks' these beautiful plans : that is why there is sin suffering disease and unese in the world.

Just like a beautiful garment disintegrates if a man un-picks the stitiches, so the beautiful blueprint of God disintegrates: As soon as man begins to 'un-think' God's beautiful plans, it all disintegrates it.

Instead of peace, there's war. Instead of love, there's fear. Instead of joy, there's pain. Instead of honor, there's envy. Instead of wealth, there's poverty.

DOUBTER

All wrongs originate in man. All wrongs originate in man's 'unpicking' of this perfect plan. And man's perfect tool he uses, is 'doubt'. Doubt is the biggest abuser of God's plan. The beautiful blueprint for earth. Every doubt in a man's mind, unpicks the perfect plan for God's perfect life for him!

ALL IN GOOD: GOOD IN ALL

God is and has, the plan or blueprint of all the lives on earth. God is the plan or blueprint of everything there is. God is not a man. God IS The Truth. God is the summation of 'all that there is'. And 'All That There Is' = G O D.

SIMPLE

Complication is unneccessary. Emotion is unnecessary. Argument is un-neccessary. If you

want the truth? .it's simple. If you need the
Truth, its here. If Truth is what is desired? Truth
will come to you.

RETRACK

Let's retrack. Where are we, in this point in
time? We are in The Age For Grace. You and I
are living in the Grace Age. The Grace Age is a
free gift where all that you need? want? and
desire? will come.

Yes: Grace is the age, where all you want,
need, require or desire, will come to you.
Repeat: Grace is the age, where all I want,
need, require or desire, will come to me!
And this age is here now!

HOW TO RECIEVE

How? By purifying our lives. If you purify your
life, you will recieve all that you need, want,
require or desire!

Yes, it is written: The pure at heart, shall see
God. In other words, The pure at heart shall

see 'good'. Good things will happen for you.
Good things are coming to you: If you will
purify and beautify your life and let this Free
gift of Grace make things happen for you!
watch and see: How life WILL work out for
you!

CHAPTER 7
WHAT ABOUT REALITY

Suddenly, I see all of America,
arising and alarmed or armed!

WHAT ABOUT REALITY

Reality is either negative or positive;
depending on what you think.
If you think positively, you will receive
positively. If you think negatively, you will
receive negatively. Simple. It is absolute truth.

ABSOLUTE TRUTH

The truth is here that God's Age of Grace is
here. What does this mean? Practically it
means the energy for good. Ever seen the
Northern Lights, seen a golden sunrise, a
silvery moon.. This phenomenal energy is like
the Grace of God. Energetic alignment for

good things to happen. Call it luck, miracles, magic or good fortune, it is all here. Right now, this time, energy is here for you to be released from your guilt.

WHY GUILT
Guilty emotions keep humans trapped. Guilty emotions detrack humans from enjoying earth life. But the gift of grace is here and you too can be set free to live your life in peace.

AFTER THE AGE OF GRACE
If we are in the age of Grace, now, where are we heading? Answer is this: After the Grace Age accomplishes everthing, it has been sent to do, a new change will come.

DESTINATION OF CREATION
Humanity is heading into The Age Of Harmony. Because, perfection is the destination of all creation; so all creation must be purifeid and beautified. What happens when humanity is purified? Humanity will be beautified? All wars will cease. All violence

will end. All poverty disipate: All disharmony will disappear. All that will remain will be of Harmony.

CHAPTER 8
WARNING

Suddenly, I see all of America,
arising and alarmed or armed!

WARNING
Our warning? Righteousness is here to stay. All
that is right will remain. All that is un-right will
be destroyed. Simple.

Ever wondered about wars, earthquakes,
violence, floods, tsunami, famines, etc etc..
Every wretchedness is being purified from the
earth! ..and no amount of politically correct
thinking can change it. So you better get
purified and beautified if you wish to survive!

YES
Yes: You better get purifed and beautified so
you can thrive. If you need help, find an R4

course. A course to reset your life and re-right your life in harmony.

First Start and rewire your emotions to solutions. Vent past hurts ad re-invent life in harmony. The result? You will fast become rich and right. You will fast be honored and adored, healthy and wealthy, excellent and excelling. This is our promise to you.

For now, remember there is a blueprint at work: Remember there is a God in control. Not the god of this world th`at wrecks havoc on this world: Not the power that steals, kills and destroys the plans of the Blueprint. No there is a better God in control.

A true God whose original purpose was for your life of peace to be joyful and fun, loveable and loving. That was the Origial plan. This Blueprint-Maker is dilligently restoring the blueprints of the earth

WHAT ON EARTH FOR?
Why is The Blueprint-Maker restoring the earth
to it's original blueprints? Why is the Blueprint-
Maker bringing creation to perfection?
Because this is the original plan. The original
destination of Creation is perfection.

Look around you and see; Can you see there is
a Blueprint maker diligently restoring the
Blueprints of the earth: Saving people from
where they are, restoring them to what they're
supposed to be. If you will allow, the
Blueprint-Maker to touch you, The Blueprint
Maker will fix you. It will fix you and restore
you to harmony.

What will the result be: Nothing less than
harmony: Delight, joy, peace, freedom will
come. It is our promise to you.

CHAPTER 9
BLUEPRINTERS

Suddenly, I see all of America,
arising and alarmed or armed!

We are blueprinters here on earth: sent to live
a life of sparkle and sound and then return to
dust. From the grave, the spirit goes back from
whence it came.

But right here, right now, you need to know
the truth: The Truth is that earth is changing.
This world is ending and a new world is
forming right aroaund you.

The world is returning to harmony. Every wish
you have wished will come true. But every
wish you have wished others as wel will come
true for you.

BEST ADVICE

Our best advice is? If you have made any bad
wishes? cancel them out now if you have
made any bad wishes for any body else?
cancel them

QUICK.

Because what ever is not cancelled out will
come to you. What evr is cancelled will be
cancelled out. What ever is forgiven you will
be forgiven others. Wht ever you forgive others
will be forgiven you!
Our best advice?
Cancel out all unforgiveness.
Our best advice?
Cancel all offences from your heart.

HARMONY TIME

A time of harmony is coming. and its good
news for those who are being saved. Good
news for you who are cancelling bad things
from their hearts; And putting in good thing in

their hearts. It is crucial. Infact it is a matter of life and death.

You have heard of karma reincarnation deja vu serendipidity.. etc. These words exist for a reason. Just because you have not identified it in your life does not mean you should ignore it. Ignore it at your peril. that is what the time of reckoning is.

CHAPTER 10
RESEEDING UNITY

Suddenly, I see all of America,
arising and alarmed or armed!

There is a need to re-seed America. When a farmer plants, a field with seeds, it fills up with crops. Seeds he sows, become plants to eat... Banana trees produce bananas? Orange trees produce oranges? Have you ever seen a Wheat seeds produce anything else but wheat?

America is sown with dis-harmony. Right now, we are eating it's fruit.

There was a time when the nation blossomed. There was peace, when there was love. There was prosperity when there was righteousness.

As a man's soul prospers, so does he prosper. As a man's soul prospers so the nation prospers. He shall increase in wealth, increase in health and increase in honor. It is written in the Book: What you sow is what you reap. If you sow good you will reap good. If you sow violence, you will reap violence. Life will not produce what it has not planted.

Look around and see: what do you see? Do you see the fields of America: See the seeds America is sown with right now? See the weeds? You like it? Why not?

WHAT CAN WE DO
Where there is dispair, let us bring hope. Where there is violence let us bring truth. where there is war, let us make peace. where there is poverty, let us bring wealth.

HOW DO WE TRANSFORM A NATION?
Education. Education is the only way a nation is transformed. Every citizen of America must be transformed by the renewing of the mind.

Each mind must be renewed. My mind must
be renewed. Your mind must be renewed.

It is the only way. No other way: Guns can not
defend us. Laws can not protect us. Rules can
not secure us. Agencies can not reach us.
Charities can not help us.

These organsations are exactly that:-
'organisations'. Organisations are 'some-
bodies', trying to organize some other bodies..
They are all bodies outside us, outside our
body. No body will protect himself more than
any body.

The exceptions? Men protecting the president.
Soon Donald Trump will be president in 2016
and men will swear to protect him. Men who
will die to protect the President of the United
States Of America.
It will be their job. They will do it with
passion. But when you think about it, they are
not doing it just for the president, they do it for
their own glory. The same sense of glory that

drives men to death in wars, in voyages, in adventures to conquer mountains, oceans, poles and space.

The honor is their glory. No man acts for any reason other than for himself, even if he goes to war and die. The complicated machinery of a human being calculates his reason for self preservation on self glorification.

No one is selfish, because everyone is selfish. No man escapes selfishness. All men are born selfish, live selfish and die selfish. Why, because it is not preservation that humans live for, it is glorification!, Every human being will do something for his own glory.

Charles Darwin's famous theory captures the essence of man. The survival of the fittest. We see that all around: But Charles Darwin missed the crucial part of the puzzle:

It is not the fittest humans that survive, other wise Olympic athletes will not die. It is not the

fittest but the passionate. We see it in
civilisations: The great civilisations thrive while
passion is high. The great civilisations advance
with passion: Humans thrive until they start to
survive. Decline begins when passion fails.
The glory begins to fade when passion fades
away.

MAGNIFICENT MOSES

The famous story of the great Israeli leader
Moses: Israel thrived gloriously under his
command. Strong mighty Moses, walked with
a shawl over his head. Why? because, of his
shining face. Golden light pouring out of his
skin and temples. Moses was no exception to
great spiritual leaders. His face was so golden,
a tea towel was needed to protect the people
from its light.

Leaders can only lead you. You have the
power to lead yourself. Dont just look to
Obama or Trump or Clinton or Putin or Assad:
Look within. Look to the God who has saved

you. By blueprinting a wonderful life for you
to lead, you get to be filled with joy and love
and peace. This is the state of harmony And in
the harmony state, you too will begin to shine
like Moses.

Yet what about all the evil in the world. Why
are people still being murdered killed lied to
deceived? It is because people are not living in
their 'harmony state' If every one was to
access their 'harmony state' they will find no
need to steal kill or destroy anything.
Yet so many are ignorant of this blueprint for a
better life. So many are ignorant of their right
to live peaceful and free. So many are living
life outside of their control.

That is why these crimes are common in the
land: adultery, perjury, idolatory,
grieviousness, disrespect, dishonour, abuse,
assault.

Guns, Laws, Rules, Agencies, Government are all outside factors. What goes on inside of you, is what you control.

Control starts by asking this question: What do I need want desire and require?

America is sown with seeds right now. Old seeds yield the conditions we see right now. But we have the chance tosow new seeds. To sow your seeds of truth. Is it time to change? Is it time to change the yields s of America? Every seed reproduces after it self.

Every fruit falls. And every fallen fruit dies. If it leaves its seed behind, new life can spring back from the ground.

Your thoughts, your words your feelings are seeds. Ask: *What am I sowing with my seeds?* Become more aware of what you feel, think say or do. These are seeds you sow.

Watch: Every seed sown always rejuvenates
and springs back as new life. Watch change
happen as your new words, new thoughts
bring new life.

IF LIFE IS BAD
We've got to change the seed. You've got to
change the seed. I've got to change the seed.
I will change me to change my country.

I am changing the seed to:....

END CHAPTER

This is not a book. This is a message.

THE AUTHOR

In pursuit of her life, what is the author's
mission but to tell the world the Truth, the
whole truth ad nothing but the Truth.

Like a lamb to slaughter, the author survived
numerous death experiences to download
these revelations crucial for our times: All in
order to tell the world. the truth in time.